Serial Killers

True Crime Tales of Cannibal Killers

By Stephanie Brannon

Table of Contents

Introduction
Inside The Mind Of A Serial Killer

Chapter 1: Jeffrey Dahmer
First murders
The Milwaukee Cannibal
1991 murder streak and arrest

Chapter 2: Metal Fang: Nikolai Dzhumagaliev
Background
Method
Career
Busted

Chapter 3: Albert Hamilton Fish: The Wolf of Wisteria
Early Life
Adulthood and increasing psychopathic tendencies
Full blown schizophrenia
Grace Budd Murder
Letters and Arrest
Revelations after Fish's arrest

Chapter 4: Karl Denke
The truth about Denke

Chapter 5: Alexander Spesivtsev

Conclusion

To the love of my life, Randall Lee. Thanks for being the most amazing husband a woman could ask for.

Introduction

Stories of crime have never failed to grip the public's attention. Acts of murder elicit widespread fear in the community and leave many questions unresolved. Authorities can spend years investigating the motive behind the crime, the planning behind it, and clues that lead to a killer's capture. While the reason for this fascination varies for each person, the story behind each act of serial murder can make for a good cautionary tale, or at least provide some moral satisfaction when justice is served.

There are mentions of crime in a variety of media, and it is justifiably disturbing to imagine similar situations where loved ones are affected. But to understand the mind of a killer, one must stand in their shoes and assess under what circumstances the murders were committed. One must determine who these people were growing up and what events took place in their lives that triggered their desire to harm innocent people.

Further speculation also reveals information about the psyche of the criminal. The motive, or lack thereof, shows under what impulse the crime was committed. Was it premeditated? Or was the individual, simply put, so 'evil' that he/she descended into depths which go against every core belief of humanity?

Some killers took the act of murder one step further, and engaged in post-mortem sex or cannibalism. For these killers, murder alone was not enough to satisfy their blood thirst desires. Their methods often involved torture, prolonged victim suffering, and dissection of corpses. For these killers, the murder itself was a means to satisfy an ulterior craving, whether for human flesh or the sight of a butchered victim.

Inside The Mind Of A Serial Killer

A serial killer is defined as an individual who murders three or more victims over a given period of time. The murders occur in a "series" and are separated by a period of "cooling off." This cooling off period is a defining characteristic found in serial killers, since they spend some time in normalcy in the period immediately following a murder. Many serial killers share similar modes of operation and target similar demographics of victims, although these parameters may not necessarily be present in a given case.

Many serial killers have also been prone to sexually abusing their victims. Overall, serial killer motives are as complex as the individuals behind the murders. Their motives range from well-thought-out schemes intended to bring change to society to more basic desires to derive pleasure, satisfaction or excitement.

Although most serial killers are found to have been affected by one or more psychological disorders, a closer look at their lives reveals an ability to hide their illnesses from the people around them. Many serial killers were known to be extremely good at pretending to be "normal," and were very cautious about their crimes lest they should be discovered. They were also known to have had a history of emotional, physical, or sexual abuse in their childhood, usually by a family member.

Such traumatic episodes can cause heavy damage to a child's psyche, making them more likely to resort to violence as adults. They torture and kill their victims in order to counteract the feeling of powerlessness that they experienced in their early development. They often engage in perverse sexual behavior and use their victims to live out their fantasies of rape, torture, and gential mutilation. Many killers evolved their violent nature over time by establishing roots of torture through animal cruelty. More than half of known serial killers have had a history of torturing and killing animals as children.

Many serial killers did not stop at murdering their victims, but would consume the flesh of their victims immediately following a kill. As horrific as it seems, it is not a new practice; cannibalism has been to known to exist for thousands of years.

In many early civilizations, the act of consuming human flesh was considered divine tradition. Human remains dating back thousands of years show evidence of human butchering and cannibalistic behavior. In modern society, cannibalism is no longer a divine practice or used in sacrificial rituals. Although humans have been known to consume human flesh in times of severe desperation, cannibalism has more recently been observed among psychologically deranged individuals who seek pleasure from the act of murder. More often than not, cannibal killers are sadistic, and often feel sexually aroused when inflicting pain upon others.

This book will shed light on the lives of real-life cannibal killers. These individuals gained infamy through the violent extent of their murders, relishing in the death of others and prolonging their victims' suffering. For these killers, the hand of death and carnal pleasure were one and the same.

Warning: The acts of violence described in this book may be harmful to certain readers and trigger unwanted thoughts or emotions. Viewer discretion is advised.

☐

Chapter 1: Jeffrey Dahmer

Known as the "Milwaukee Cannibal," Jeffrey Dahmer is perhaps the most famous cannibal serial killer of the 20th century. He sexually assaulted and murdered 17 people over a period of 13 years. He indulged in necrophilia, and also consumed various body parts of some of his victims. His sexual inclination was that of a homosexual and he enacted various perverted fantasies with his victims in an extremely disturbing manner. He was also charged with child molestation and indecent exposure.

On May 21, 1960, a couple in West Allis, Wisconsin were blessed with a son. Joyce Dahmer was the mother, and the father Lionel Dahmer was a student of Chemistry at Marquette University. Jeffrey was a cheerful child in his younger years, but he gradually became reserved. His parents were always busy with work, and he received little attention from them.

After his brother was born, he felt neglected and became withdrawn. His parent's marriage was not a happy one. There were regular arguments as his mother demanded more and more attention from Lionel Dahmer. She was often admitted to the mental hospital and regularly abused prescription pills. With his parents not giving him time, Jeffrey manifested an obsession for dead animals. He was curious about how every animal "fitted together." He began collecting bones from carcasses he found on the roadside, eventually killing the animals himself to collect their bones. He asked his father how to bleach and preserve bones. Lionel, thinking that his son was taking interest in chemistry, was more than happy to teach Jeffrey.

By the time he was in high school, Dahmer had developed into an alcoholic. He had discovered by then that he was homosexual. The pressure of fitting in and the tension between his parents at home contributed heavily towards his alcoholism. After getting drunk, Dahmer would fantasize about raping and exercising dominance in a sexual encounter. His parents went through a bitter divorce as he graduated from high school. He was living alone in their family house during this time.

First murders

Jeffrey killed his first victim within a couple weeks of graduating from high school, on June 18, 1978. He picked up Steven Hicks, a 19-year-old hitchhiker, and took him to his family's house. After spending hours drinking with Dahmer, Hicks decided to leave. The constant feeling of abandonment had been haunting him all his life, and Hicks' decision reminded

Jeffrey of it. To prevent him from leaving, Dahmer hit him in the head with a dumbbell. When his guest had passed out, he strangled him to death with the dumbbell. He then stripped Hicks's clothes off and masturbated over his corpse. He then dismembered his remains the following day, and with great skill dissolved the flesh in acid and crushed the bones to dust with a sledgehammer before discarding it in the woods.

Dahmer was accepted to Ohio State University, from which he dropped out shortly thereafter, owing to his drinking problems. He returned home, where his father urged him to join the army. He was trained as a medical specialist and was posted in Germany. His alcoholism got the best of him there too, and he was soon discharged from the army. He was deemed unfit for the service, so he was discharged with honors. He returned to West Allis.

After spending a few years working here and there, getting arrested for comparatively minor offenses like drunk and disorderly conduct, indecent exposure, and child molestation, he moved in to live with his grandmother. He finally got a job at the Milwaukee chocolate factory. One day, he met a man named Steven Tuomi at a bar. He picked up the 25-year-old and took him to the Ambassador Hotel. Dahmer could not recall what followed that night, but when he woke up the next morning, he realized that he had killed Tuomi. He had crushed his chest and had absolutely no memory of it. He moved the dead body out of the hotel in a large suitcase. He dissected Tuomi's body after a few days and disposed of it in the trash after carving the flesh into smaller, manageable pieces. However, he had saved the severed head to preserve the skull. He bleached the skull bone and used it for masturbation before crushing the skull and disposing of the remains.

This murder had given Dahmer satisfaction, and he eventually started hunting for victims, finding the perfect opportunity to commit another grisly murder. Two months later, he found a 14-year-old boy named James Doxtator. He offered the boy money to pose naked for pictures. James went with him to his house, where Dahmer strangled him after sexual activity. The remains were taken care of in the same way as before. His next victim was a 22-year-old man named Richard Guerrero, whom he lured back to his place in similar fashion as before. There, he drugged Richard only to kill him by strangling. He then performed fellatio on the dead body before disposing of it. After murdering him, he was arrested for molesting a 13-year-old boy named Somsack Sinthasomphone. Dahmer was booked as a registered sex offender and was released in a few days.

The gruesomeness of Dahmer's crimes reached a new high with his fifth victim, Anthony Sears. The two met at a gay bar on March 25, 1989. After spending the evening talking and drinking together, Dahmer took Sears back to his grandmother's house. They indulged in oral sex before he killed Sears by strangling him. In later interviews, Dahmer claimed that he had really liked Sears, and so he decided to preserve his skull, scalp and genitalia. He took care of the rest of the body by stripping the skin off the flesh and dissolving it in acid. By the end of that year, Dahmer moved out of his grandmother's house and started living in Milwaukee.

The Milwaukee Cannibal

Shortly after moving into his new house, Dahmer killed a male prostitute, Raymond Smith. Smith was at his place to spend the night with him, and he was killed after being drugged. Dahmer strangled the 32-year-old man with his bare hands this time. In the next few days, Jeffrey thoroughly used and enjoyed his newly claimed prize, the corpse. He took photos of the body in various poses before butchering it into pieces. He preserved

Raymond's skull, and spray painted it before displaying it alongside his other possessions.

Dahmer spent three months "cooling off" from the previous crime. His next victim was 22-year-old Ernest Miller, whom he drugged upon reaching home. He wanted to be creative with his method of killing this time, as he was getting used to the violence and the excitement was running thin. He slit Miller's throat with a knife and watched him bleed to death. Using a Polaroid camera, Dahmer took photos of the dead body in various provocative poses. He severed the head to preserve the skull, which he painted with enamel after bleaching. He also preserved the heart, biceps and pieces of flesh from the legs in his refrigerator so he could eat them at a later time. He believed that if he ate his victims, they would be a part of him forever. He then killed and ate various body parts of another 22-year-old man named David Thomas. He strangled Thomas to death and took several photos of the naked corpse. The next few months were spent in unsuccessful attempts at luring young men back to his place. Dahmer's probation officer at the time recalls him being unhappy and depressed. He hadn't felt the satisfaction he longed for in a long time.

1991 murder streak and arrest

By this point, Jeffrey Dahmer had not found a victim in a long time. In Dahmer's mind, murder had become a necessity. In February 1991, he found 17-year-old Curtis Straughter at a bus stop and offered him money for sex and naked photos. After the said activities, Curtis was strangled with a leather strap, after which his corpse was used for sexual activities and eventually castrated. Dahmer preserved the skull, hands and genitals and disposed of the rest of the body. He also made an attempt to retain the skin of the victim, but he failed in that respect. Dahmer had become increasingly obsessed with preserving the corpses as best as he could, so he began devising a new method of killing. After a couple of months, Dahmer was prepared. He only had to hunt for another prize to add to his collection.

Errol Lindsey was a 19-year-old heterosexual he met on the street. He took the boy to his apartment where he drugged him before drilling a hole into his skull. His new method also included pouring muriatic acid into the skull. Even so, this new experiment did not kill Errol. He woke up a few hours later complaining of a headache when Dahmer strangled him. He then went on to engage in necrophilia, and then dexterously flayed the corpse to preserve the skin. He retained the skull and disposed of the rest of the body in the usual manner.

Coincidentally, he met Konerak Sinthasomphone, younger brother of Somsack whom Dahmer had molested three years ago. He took the 14-year-old home to sexually abuse him before drilling two holes into his skull and pouring muriatic acid into them. The boy escaped while Dahmer was out drinking beer, only to run back into him when he returned from the bar. Dahmer successfully convinced the policemen who were called that Konerak was actually his 19-year-old lover, and brought him back home again. The police escorted them to the apartment without a shred of doubt, since Dahmer claimed the boy was too intoxicated to say anything. He died when he was injected with more muriatic acid as soon as the police left, his body used as per Dahmer's sexual fantasies. He preserved the boy's skull.

Next month, while on a trip to Chicago Dahmer met Matt Turner at a bus station and offered him money to travel to Milwaukee for a photo shoot. Matt accepted the offer, only to get strangled and dismembered at the apartment. His head, internal organs and torso were preserved. Within a week, he had found yet another victim. Jeremiah Weinberger met him in Chicago and was visiting Milwaukee to see Jeffrey. When he met Dahmer at his home, he was drugged and had a hole drilled into his skull. Dahmer injected boiling water into the hole twice, from which Weinberger died after being comatose for a couple of days.

After a fortnight, Dahmer met his next victim, 24-year-old Oliver Lacy. He brought him to his house where he drugged and killed Lacy by strangling him to death. He engaged in necrophilia with the corpse and preserved the head, heart and the skeletons in the refrigerator. He ate flesh from his right bicep and placed the body in a vat. He killed his last victim, Joseph Bradehoft a week later in a similar manner before preserving the dismembered remains in the same vat.

The Cannibal of Milwaukee was arrested the next week when one of his victims, Tracy Edwards escaped from his house and reported the incident to the police. Police officers came down to his house to investigate the matter and found pictures of various corpses that Dahmer had took. A detailed search later brought up seven skulls, two human hearts, an entire torso and a bag of assorted human flesh wrapped up in the freezer. They also found two whole sets of human skeletons, severed hands and genitalia, and three bodies left dissolving in acid. What followed was a case covered heavily by the media around the world, leading Jeffrey to be indicted following his confessions of the crime. He proclaimed himself to be born again and accepted that he knew he was doing something evil owing to his mental illness. He pled guilty by reason of insanity but was eventually deemed to be sane by the court. He was sentenced to 16 life sentences at the Columbia Correctional Institution.

On November 28, 1994, Dahmer was murdered by fellow inmate, Christopher Scarver. Dahmer suffered severe trauma to the head after being bludgeoned by a metal bar. He was found lying on the bathroom floor of the prison, still alive, but died hours later after being rushed to the hospital. Scarver claimed that he had confronted Dahmer about his crimes, and that Dahmer was disliked by the other inmates. After beating Dahmer to the ground, Scarver returned to his cell and told the prison guard that "God told me to do it."

Many of Dahmer's interviews point to one fact: his fondness of necrophilia and cannibalism began at the early age of 14. It was triggered by unfortunate events at home when his parents' marriage took a turn for the worst, eventually leading to a divorce. Dahmer was a closet homosexual who couldn't get a grip on his sexuality. He ended up resorting to murder, necrophilia and cannibalism at an early age, taking the lives of 17 unsuspecting victims. Whether a loving upbringing and acceptance from society would have altered the outcome of his life is a common topic of speculation for those interested in Dahmer's life.

☐

Chapter 2: Metal Fang: Nikolai Dzhumagaliev

Nikolai Dzhumagaliev is a Soviet cannibal serial killer who remains imprisoned to this day. He is instantly recognizable by his metal teeth, which he received after his actual teeth were knocked off in a fight. His metal teeth also contributed to the nickname 'Metal Fang' which he received after attaining widespread notoriety from his killings. The cunning serial killer managed to escape police custody eight years after his initial imprisonment, but was recaptured in 1991. Dzhumagaliev reportedly committed the murders and cannibalism of ten people during 1979 to 1980. However, since his initial capture, more than a hundred murders have been alleged upon Dzhumagaliev.

Nikolai Dzhumagaliev was born on November 15, 1952. He was born and brought up in Uzynagash which lies in modern-day Kazakhstan, erstwhile Kazakh SSR. He was the only son of a Kazakh father and a Belarusian mother. He had three other sisters. Nikolai joined a railway school after completing his primary education and was soon assigned a job in Atyrau. Soon in 1970, Nikolai got conscripted into the Soviet Army, serving in the Chemical Defence Department at Samarkand, Uzbek SSR. After serving his time in the Soviet Army, Nikolai Dzhumagaliev returned with hopes of entering university to pursue further education. This did not work out owing to circumstances at that time. He also fancied becoming a full-time driver, however, this plan also did not work out well for Nikolai and he soon left the city dejected. He traveled extensively in the Soviet Union spending a lot of solitary time in Siberia as well as the Ural Mountains. He also spent some time in Murmansk where he flitted in and out of several professions such as a sailor, a bulldozer driver, a forwarder and even an electrician. He returned to his home in Uzynagash in the Kazakh SSR in the year of 1977. It was during this year that Nikolai contracted syphilis and trichomoniasis. Barely a year after that in January of 1979, Nikolai committed his first murder. The incident took place in the desolate and sparse countryside of Uzynagash. His victim was a peasant woman who met her fateful and gruesome death just around the street corner while returning to her home in the evening. Nikolai gave a chilling description of this murder when he confessed to his crimes after being caught by the authorities. He described the entire incident like a hunting scene. His tale was chilling and bloody. He wanted to experience the joys and wonders of man hunting and hence he committed murder upon the innocent woman. Nikolai found his victim walking alone on the deserted Uzung-agach-Maibulak track. As the victim was walking back to her home, she turned around to find Nikolai running after her with a mad look on his face. He proceeded to grab her from behind and upon the woman's protests; he slit her throat with his pocket knife. He then dragged the peasant woman to a landfill site where it was difficult to be spotted. Interestingly, as he stood next to the corpse immediately after the kill, the village bus drove down the street. Nikolai fell down on top of the woman's body to avoid being seen and the bus drove away not noticing them in the dark. What followed was an act of utter horror and cold-blooded schizophrenia. Nikolai went ahead and stripped the woman's corpse naked. He then cut the victim' breasts and carefully took out the ovaries of the dead woman. He also cut away her hips and pelvis which he carefully packed in his bag. He then took his prized meat home to feast upon the flesh and meat of a woman. He ate the meat in a variety of manners. He grilled some of the pieces, roasted some, and fried a select few pieces.

Nikolai never shared this meat and considered it as an exclusive delicacy reserved for himself alone. He melted the human fat which he had retrieved from the woman's corpse along with a select few pieces of her body. Nikolai even made pickles from small chunks of the woman's meat which he occasionally consumed with his meals. He even minced portions of the meat in his meat grinder and made dumplings out of them. This was just the start of many more innocent victims who fell prey to Nikolai's cravings for human flesh. In his confessions, Nikolai recalled how he had found the heart and the liver pieces of the woman's meat to be too tough and had to grill them in the woman's fat in order to soften the texture.. But he also remarked that he enjoyed ripping through tough meat immediately following an exhilarating kill.

That same year Nikolai was reported to make another six kills in the area. He was a calculated killer, often planning his hunt carefully in mind before attempting the act. Nikolai claimed that he often hosted parties at his home and invited friends over for dinner. During such macabre parties, Nikolai fed his unknowing guests the human meat from his hunting expeditions. To Nikolai, the act of cannibalism was a sadistic and cruel pleasure that he wanted others to accept as a societal norm.

Background

Nikolai was known as a clean-shaven gentleman who generally kept to himself. Nikolai had friends in his social and professional circles and appeared to be an amicable young man by people who knew him.

In fact, when it was revealed that he was a cannibal killer who feasted upon the bodies of women, Nikolai's friends and neighbors were all shocked. Nikolai, unlike other serial killers and cannibals, had a peaceful and ordinary childhood. He was always neatly dressed and committed to his work. Nothing seemed strange in his personality to make an inkling of his psychopathic nature. Nikolai was in many respects, the real-life Hannibal Lector. He was calm and he was composed. He was also very articulate about his killings and made no one suspect of his motivations and behavioral tendencies until he was discovered. People around him were more than eager to look past the only physical deformity he had. He had replaced most of his teeth with metallic dentures after his teeth had been knocked out in a brawl. He often threw dinner parties which were attended by people from the town. It was at these parties that Nikolai would serve platters of food for his guests, some containing human flesh as the main ingredient.

Method

Nikolai planned out his murders and the after actions very carefully in advance. He had constructed himself a mental theory when he wanted to rid the society of all unfaithful women as well as the one who were selling their body and mind for money. He was out there to eliminate all the prostitutes from the world. Even though he was convicted of a few seven murders in all, he is believed to be responsible for over one hundred murders during that time. All his victims were women who Nikolai claimed were infidels. He used to follow women into a hidden park near a waterfront. This was not hard considering his polished and calm looks. He then roped them and cut them into pieces with a Hachette or a short axe which he used to carry along with him to the park. He would go on to sexually assault his victim's corpse before chopping off their body parts with surgical precision. The body parts were the prize of his hunt. He would bring different parts of the body chopped up to his home and stored them in his refrigerator. He served some of this meat to unsuspecting dinner party guests.

Career

Nikolai's first victim was Nadezhda Yerofiz. He killed Nadezhda, dismembered her and threw away her remains in an empty barrel lying down the street. The following year he killed another woman returning from the church. This murder was uncovered by the police who managed to find the remains of the woman's body and Nikolai was arrested. After spending close to a year in the jail, Nikolai was declared legally insane after some medical tests were carried on him by the prison authorities. He was diagnosed with schizophrenia.

He was released from the prison following his diagnosis and he started working as a farm laborer in the town of Alma-Ata which was near his own hometown. Soon in 1980, Nikolai launched into another killing spree which lasted for over a year before he was discovered and arrested again by the police. Nikolai was a deeply rooted misogynist who believed every woman to be a harlot and engaging in prostitution. In his view, women were a menace to society and needed to be eradicated from the world. He believed he was doing a service of charity to the world by killing and hunting down women one by one. Nikolai had a distinct hatred for European women whom he had encountered during his time in the military. The European women appeared to be 'too free' and 'too promiscuous' in Nikolai's mind.

Nikolai Dzhumagaliev confessed that he would sometimes hide behind rocks, looking for potential victims as they crossed his path. On one occasion, Nikolai captured a woman and dragged her behind his hiding spot. He cut her throat and drank her blood until the blood was completely drained from the woman's neck. He then proceeded to have sex with the woman's corpse. What followed was his typical cannibalistic ritual. He savored every bit of the woman's flesh while saving her heart and other organs for special occasions.

After each successful hunt of his female victims, Nikolai organized barbecue dinner parties at his home. Included on the menu were dishes consisting of his most recent kills. Nikolai admitted that a single kill would give him enough meat to last him two weeks. He would become sexually aroused by watching his innocent friends feast upon human meat unknowingly.

Busted

Nikolai was eventually apprended by police at one of his dinner parties. He invited over two people to his home for a barbecue one evening. The two people accidently chanced upon a woman's bloody head hanging in Nikolai's kitchen while he was preparing her intestines for dinner. They soon brought in the police and Nikolai's heinous criminal trajectory was revealed to the public. The arrest was made in 1981. During his interrogation Nikolai was linked to over a hundred murders, most of which he admitted to.

His medical examination once again revealed mental instability. Nikolai was tried on seven counts of first-degree murder. He was shifted to a mental institution where he attempted committing suicide on two occassions.

After being treated for a few years in the mental institutions, the doctors found that Nikolai's mental disorder had been improved and that he could be shifted to another hospital. The doctors deemed him not to be of any threat to society. Because of his improved condition, Nikolai was not escorted by security guards to his new ward. Nikolai used this as an opportunity to escape the hospital, and in 1989 he fled into the Kyrgyzstan mountains.

Nikolai was found again by the Russian police in 1991. The details of his activity during the two years of his escape is not available. There is no knowledge whether Nikolai killed more women during this time or kept a low profile to evade being captured. In fact, his initial escape from the hospital in 1989 was never publicly reported due to fear that it would create widespread panic.

According to Russian sources, Nikolai is now held in a secret high-security psychiatric ward but there have been reports of a second escape on December 23, 2015. However, the local Russian police have no information regarding the psychopath's second bid at freedom.

Chapter 3: Albert Hamilton Fish: The Wolf of Wisteria

Albert Hamilton Fish was born on May, 19th 1870 and was electrocuted to death on January 16th, 1936 after being tried on multiple counts of murder, molestation and cannibalism in the United States. He was known as the Werewolf of Wisteria and the Brooklyn Vampire in popular culture and urban legends. He was a prolific and a perverted killer who was sexually driven to commit murder and perform lacerations upon the corpse. He claimed to have eaten and molested children in every state. Fish eventually confessed three murders to the police and admitted to having stabbed two victims during his interrogation.

Early Life

Fish was born in Washington DC and grew up with three other siblings in the family. His family had a history of mental illness. His brothers and sisters had both been diagnosed with mental illnesses while his uncle had suffered from mania. Fish's mother would often experience aural or visual hallucinations. When Fish was a child, his father died of heart attack and his mother had to put the young boy in an orphanage. It was at the orphanage where Fish became a victim of abuse, trauma, and countless experiences that would affect him for the rest of his life. Fish was sexually abused at the orphanage and also experienced regular physical torture. The boys were often stripped naked and whipped by the orphanage management. During night time, the boys would sexually abuse younger boys in the orphanage. Fish began to enjoy the pain he was subjected to. Perhaps his mental stability was shaken forever. It was too late by the time Fish's mother Ellen managed to secure a government job and take her son Hamilton out from the orphanage. When Hamilton Fish was twelve years of age, he was introduced to a telegraph boy in Washington. He started a sexually perverse relationship with the boy and practiced urolagnia (drinking urine) and coprophagia (eating feces). He used to frequent the public baths of the town where he would stand behind unnoticed and spied on boys while they took a bath. He felt sexually aroused by his voyeuristic adventures.

Adulthood and increasing psychopathic tendencies

As Fisher grew, his psychopathic and sick mentality also grew with him. In 1898, his mother arranged a marriage for him with a young woman, and the couple would go to have six children. At all points of time in his marriage, Fish was engaged in perverse sexual relationships with many people, mostly young boys. He worked as a prostitute and had started torturing some of his customers already. On one occasion, he took a nineteen-year-old boy named Thomas Kedden to a barn. Fish was having a sexual relationship with him but what awaited Thomas that fateful night was truly horrific. Fish took his partner to an abandoned farmhouse. After engaging in sexual acts with the boy, Fish went on to tie him up and mutilate his penis. He cut off half of Kedden's penis with a razor blade as the boy screamed in vain. He had planned to kill Thomas after his sexual experiment and mutilation was complete but it was summer season and Fish worried that the stench of a dead corpse would emanate in the summer heat. Fish decided to sterilize the victim's mutilated penis with Vaseline and antiseptic, and after doctoring the wound, he left on a train and never heard from the boy again. Fish claimed that his fascination with the mutilation of genitals began with a trip he once took to the waxworks museum, where he saw a bisection of the human penis.

In 1917, Fish's wife left him, forcing him raise his six children as a single father. He never engaged in physical abuse or sexual molestation with his kids but often encouraged them to spank his butt with a steel studded leather belt. Fish often prepared himself a dinner which would consist of solely raw meat. He sometimes gave his children the meat to eat as well so they could develop a taste for tough meat. This was also the time when his fascination with self-harm was rekindled and he often practiced hitting himself with belts and steel studded nails in the behind until he would bleed. From 1917 to 1920 Fish's children reported him having recurring auditory and visual hallucinations. He was slowly losing his composure and sanity. At one point, he wrapped himself up in a carpet rug and started proclaiming that he was working on the orders of John the Apostle. Fish also inserted needles and metal pins in his groin and anus. This was something he would go on to do with many of his future child victims. After his arrest, he was examined medically and his x-rays showed thirty metal pins stuck inside his abdomen. Fish was initially using the needles to pick the skin off his groin but slowly he started inserting them to the point where he could no longer take them out.

Full blown schizophrenia

In the years following 1919, Fish's condition worsened and he became increasingly violent. He would target weak and helpless people who could hardly defend themselves from his attack. He had a carefully planned course of action. His victims were mostly children and handicapped or mentally challenged people. Fish also targeted African Americans because he felt that their absence would not get noticed easily since they were in the lower rungs of the society.

During this time, Fish had assembled an arsenal of horrific weapons of torture, or what he liked to call the "Implements of Hell." Fish's "Implements of Hell" consisted of a butcher's knife, a meat cleaver and a portable hand saw. Fish was suffering from full blown psychosis during this time. He believed that he had experienced a divine revelation from God himself. He was divinely commissioned to killing, mutilating and sexually torturing children.

Grace Budd Murder

In 1928, Fish posed as Frank Howard and visited a young man named Edward Budd who had put up an ad offering his services in the country. Fish claimed to be a wealthy farm owner and offered Budd a job to work on his farm, secretly intending to mutilate the young boy and leave him bleeding to death. When he was at the residence of Budd he saw his little sister, Grace. Fish immediately became drawn towards the child. He abandoned his plans to castrate Edward Budd and instead began to devise a plan to mutilate the body of the young girl. He had lavishly offered jobs not just to Edward Budd but also his friend Willie. The boys were excited at the handsome salary they had been offered by Fish, posing under the guise of farm owner Frank Howard.

Frank promised the Budd's that he would return the next day and pick both of the boys up so they could start working on his farm. Before leaving, Howard offered little Grace to come along with him to his sister's niece's birthday party. He cajoled her parents that she could have some fun for a change. Grace put on her favorite coat and left with Frank Howard. When Grace's parents asked where he would take her, Fish gave them a fake address and promised to return her safely before nine in the evening.

Sadly, Grace would never return home again. That evening there was no word from Mr. Frank Howard. Following a rather anxious and sleepless night, young Edward went to the police in the morning to officially report the missing of Grace Budd. Police soon revealed to the Budd family that it was a hoax all along. The address of Howard's sister which he had given to Grace's parents was fictitious. The old man was a fraud.

It was nearly June and there was still no trace of Grace Budd or her body. It was as if she had disappeared from the face of the earth along with the strange old man. The police circulated thousands of posters of Mr. Howard along with a description given by Edward Budd and assigned more than twenty detectives to solve the case. After his arrest, Fish testified to his attorney that he had no intentions of raping Grace Budd, but also admitted to having ejaculated twice while strangling the little girl.

Letters and Arrest

After capturing Grace Budd, Fish took her to an empty house in Westchester, where he strangled her to death and ate her remains. He decided to write an obscene letter which gave details of the torture and murder of little Grace Budd. He addressed the letter to the child's mother. Because Budd's mother was illiterate, her son was forced to read the letter to her. As soon as he finished reading he ran to the police department and handed them the letter, hoping it could provide a lead in the case and help track down the psychopath killer.

The letter indeed provided to be the lead which led the police department to locate the killer. Fish was clever enough to use an alias to send the letter and keep his identity anonymous, but he made a critical error. He used the stationary of a Western Union office in Manhattan which helped the police to track him down. He was apprehended by detective William F. King.

King asked Fish to accompany him to the police station for questioning. Fish initially agreed but then brandished a sharp razor blade and attacked the chief investigating officer. King tactfully managed to overpower the murderer and took him into custody. Fish confessed to his crimes soon after.

By the time Fish was finally apprehended, it was impossible to determine exactly how many victims he had claimed. The case of Grace Budd remained unsolved for a period of six years, from her initial disappearance in 1928 until 1934. The letter came in an envelope which bore a tiny N.Y.P.C.B.A. logo which belonged to the New York Chauffeur's Private Benevolent Association. King immediately conducted a handwriting test on every member of the office. Every member of the association passed the test. The only potential lead seemed to have met a dead end. King then made a thorough inquiry about any person who had taken the office stationary out of the premises. A janitor admitted to have taken and left behind few envelopes at his lodge at 200 East 52nd Street. When King questioned the rooming house's landlady, he learned that a man of exactly Howard's description had been living in one of the lodge's rooms up until a month prior. He had left the residence citing without explanation and without providing a new address. But there was still one hope alive in this case. The old man had mentioned to the landlady that he was expecting a money order which was to be delivered soon to his room in the lodge. The letter had yet not arrived. King instructed the landlady to hold Fish's letter and call him immediately when he showed up to collect his money order. The plan worked and on December 13th, 1934, Officer King received a call from the landlady that the suspect had arrived to take his letter and was in his room. When King reached the place he found Fish sitting in his room peacefully with a teacup in his hand. He was arrested soon after he tried to attack the police officer with a razor.

Here is an excerpt from the letter which Albert Fish wrote to Grace Budd's parents:

"You said yes she could go. I took her to an empty house in Westchester I had already picked out. When we got there, I told her to remain outside. She picked wildflowers. I went upstairs and stripped all my clothes off. I knew if I did not I would get her blood on them. When all was ready I went to the window and called her. Then I hid in a closet until she was in the room. When she saw me all naked she began to cry and tried to run downstairs. I grabbed her and she said she would tell her mama. First I stripped her naked. How she did kick – bite and scratch. I choked her to death then cut her in small pieces so I could take my meat to my rooms, cook and eat it. How sweet and tender her little ass was roasted in the oven. It took me 9 days to eat her entire body. I did not fuck her, though; I could of, had I wished. She died a virgin."

Fish was charged with the murder and mutilation of Grace Budd. He admitted to having killed her and gave a spine-chilling account to add to his confession. He admitted to taking Grace to an abandoned two storied building called 'The Wisteria Cottage' in the middle of woody area. Fish asked Grace to look at the wildflowers growing outside the cottage while he prepared his 'Implements of Hell.' After beheading the child, Fish undressed her and carefully chopped up pieces of her body with his butcher's knife. He packed parts of the meat in a newspaper which he took home to eat. He threw the remains of the body behind the stone walls of the Wisteria Cottage which was recovered by the police after Fish's arrest. When Budd's family was called to identify the criminal, King was certain that they had caught the 'boogey man' of Brooklyn.

Revelations after Fish's arrest

Four-year-old Bill Gaffney was kidnapped on February 11th, 1927 from the Brooklyn Trolley line. A motorman had seen an old man dragging away a crying boy who did not have a coat on. When Fish was asked about his relation to the incident, he confessed to having done unspeakable things to the boy. The 'Boogey Man' confessed to the police that he took Bill to the River Avenue dumping grounds. On the premises was an empty house, where Fish would keep the boy alive for the next day. He stripped Bill naked and tied his hands and feet. He gagged him so that he would not make any noise. Bill's clothes and shoes were burnt by Fish in the dumping ground. Fish then proceeded to return to his home as if nothing had happened. The following noon Fish returned to the house in the River Avenue Dumps armed with his 'Implements of Hell'. Fish also made a heavy cat of nine tails at his home by cutting his leather belt into nine strips and fixing a short handle to it. The torture whip was about eight inches long. Fish whipped Bill's bottom with his improvised cat of nine tails until the child's bottom bled. He then cut the child's ears and nose with his razor blade. Bill's mouth was slit from his ear to ear. By this time, the child was dead. Fish then gouged out Bill's eyeballs and stuck a knife in his belly right below his belly button. Fish then put his mouth to the wound and drank as much blood as he could from the body. The cannibal killer then proceeded to cut the dead body carefully in pieces. The inedible pieces such as the lower part of the child's limbs and the head were collected in a gunny sack which was filled with heavy stones. Fish collected the other parts of the dead body that he would eat at his home. These pieces included the soft cartilage of the ears and the nose. Before leaving the scene, Fish took the gunny sack filled with Bill's remains and tossed it into the bottom of a slimy pool at the end of the road.

Fish further confessed to having cooked the boy's body parts like the rear and genitals in his oven. He made a stew of his ears, nose and other cartilages along with celery, salt, pepper and spring onions. Fish prepared a rather elaborate dish of the boy's genitals and his bottom. He cut open the butt cheeks in two, slicing them with his sharp knife. Then he put strips of bacon and cheese on each butt cheek. The genitals were also washed and sliced and added to the dish. The meat was then dressed in salt and pepper and placed in the oven for roasting. The meat was prodded with a wooden spoon at regular intervals to make it cook nice and even without charring. Fish claimed that the time taken to fully roast the child's rear was about two hours and he consumed every bit of Gaffney's meat in about four days.

Fish was charged with a third count of homicide when he was convicted of murdering a fifteen-year-old girl named Mary O'Connor in the Far Rockaway. He had mauled and strangled the girl in a woody area close to where she lived. Mary's dead body was discovered by her family a day after she was murdered by Albert Fish.

Fish confessed to another murder of an eleven-year-old boy named Francis McDonald. He had picked up the child when he was playing catch with his friends in the Port Richmond neighborhood of Staten Island. The incident occurred in 1924 but it was only in March 1935, after having being convicted of the murder of Grace Budd that Albert Fish admitted to having murdered the eleven-year-old boy as well.

Chapter 4: Karl Denke

Affectionately known as "papa" by his tenants, Karl Denke's arrest for attacking a man with an axe shocked his entire community. He had never shown any kind of aggression in his behavior before and they did not believe it at first. Little did they know that this attack was the least surprising thing about their beloved landlord. A thorough search of his house by the police revealed human flesh stored in large jars of curing salt. In a ledger, Denke had enlisted the names of the 40 people he had murdered and cannibalized over a period of time.

There is a scarcity of information about his early life, but there is enough information to piece out the fact that Denke was dull child suspected to be retarded. He operated a rooming house and was a devout Christian who never missed a day at the church. His silent demeanor and his occasional philanthropy earned him the name "Papa Denke." His only source of income was the rent his tenants paid him.

The story of Denke's grisly life first came to light when he was charged for attacking a man named Vincenz Oliver with an axe. When questioned by police, Denke claimed that he was defending himself against Oliver, believing him to be a burglar. After just two days of confinement however, Denke hanged himself in his jail cell. A police team was then sent to his house to further investigate the matter. There, they found pieces of human flesh and bones preserved in salt solution. Reports revealed that he dismembered and preserved his victims within a few hours of murdering them. There was also evidence of human flesh being cooked in cream sauce. More bones were found in his shed, from where the meat had been consumed and the bones cleaned. More than three hundred teeth were also discovered, where they were sorted according to size and preserved.

The truth about Denke

Denke's modus operandi involved inviting beggars and vagabonds around the nearby train station to his home. He offered them shelter and food for a nominal cost at his rooming house. He would attack them with an axe once they were at his place and would later dismember their bodies into a number of smaller pieces. He enjoyed the taste of human flesh himself, and also gave it to his tenants after cooking. There is also evidence suggesting that he used to sell human meat as pork in the nearby markets.

To this day, there is little known about his motives behind the murders and his cannabalistic behavior. One theory suggests that he did it out of desperation in order to have enough to eat. It was a time of recession in Germany and starvation was prevalent. He had failed in his attempts at farming and market stocks. The result was a killing spree, after which he never lacked meat for food even at the worst times. His neighbors believed him to have been consuming dog meat. Although forbidden, it was not that big of a deal for them. The case of Denke never garnered much attention from the public because of multiple factors. He had already killed himself in police custody, and reports of his cannibalism made it an uncomfortable topic of conversation.

There has been speculation as to the reason for why Denke was never caught. It was later discovered that two of his previous victims had escaped after being hit with an axe. Surprisingly, the matter was not brought to the attention of police. One possible explanation was his unsuspecting demeanor. Denke was perceived as being a dull and slow person who could have never committed such atrocities. Furthermore, the allegations against him were brought up by beggars and vagabonds who weren't easily trusted. Denke's establishment provided cheap housing without asking his tenants many questions. He depended on his reputation in the town to convince people to free him of the doubts and suspicion. The estimated 40 victims are based solely on the information contained in a ledger he himself maintained. His case is truly intriguing, all the more because of the lack of detailed information about his victims and his motives.

☐

Chapter 5: Alexander Spesivtsev

Better known as the "Siberian Ripper," Alexander Nikolayevich Spesivtsev lived in the Siberian town of Novokuznetsk with his mother Lyudmila. From 1991 to 1996, he murdered and cannibalized more than 80 victims, out which he confessed to committing 19 of them, and was only convicted for 4 murders. His victims were mostly street children from the less fortunate section of the society.

He was born in 1970 in a disturbed household. He was tortured and beaten by his father as a child. His only support was his mother, with whom he had an unusual relation with. His mother would tell him stories of murder at bedtime and show him pictures of corpses from a very early age. He soon got accustomed to violence and developed sadistic tendencies. He committed his first murder at the young age of 18, after which he was admitted to a mental hospital. But he was released shortly after. He moved into an apartment with his mother and a Doberman, where together they lured in and murdered a number of victims.

His mother would lure children into their house, promising them food, clothes and shelter. Once they had been lured in,

Spesivtsev stabbed them from behind. He did not kill his victims swiftly, rather he watched them bleed to death from the multiple stab wounds he had inflicted on them.

Despite several complaints of a rotten smell around Alexander's apartment and the loud rock music played in his house all throughout the day, the police continued to ignore the matter. They thought it was simple case of a die hard rock fan living in unhygienic conditions. There were, however, no complaints from his neighbors regarding the disappearance of street kids, and none of them suspected that a murderer was amongst them.

When police discovered a dismembered body part floating in the river, they conducted an investigation into the possibility of a serial killer on the loose. It was at this point that police finally paid some attention to the complaints of stench around Alexander's house. The authorities found blood splattered all over the walls, floors and even the ceiling. The entire house was scattered with dead remains of multiple victims, with human flesh stuck to the utensils. A rib cage lay on the floor in the living room, and the bathroom had a headless corpse in it.

A fifteen-year-old Olga Galtseva was found in his house in a battered and mutilated state. She died on the way to the hospital after telling the police about the incident. She and a couple of her friends were asked by Lyudmila to carry some bags inside the house. They were ambushed by Alexander as soon as they entered, where he raped all of them. He killed one of the girls after sexually abusing her for quite a while and made the other two girls cut up her body. His Doberman killed the second girl while his mother cooked the cut up corpse of the first one. They fed on the meat, and force fed Olga the dead remains of her friend before stabbing her repeatedly.

Alexander and Lyudmila were soon arrested by the police. There he admitted his guilt while his mother denied any involvement. On trial, however, they were both booked as murderer and accomplice and were sentenced to life imprisonment. The motive for the murders, as stated by him during the trial, was to clean the world of the "filth" that those poor children represented. He blamed Russia's democracy and negligence to the widespread poverty prevalent in the country. He hated the country for not paying attention to the state of its citizens and killed the children who were to him a constant reminder of the country's plight. Even if he could justify his brutal murders as an attack on the state of the nation, he could not explain his acts of sexual abuse and cannibalism against his victims. While his mother did not kill any of the victims, she was the one who lured, cut up and cooked the bodies. Although Alexander was found to be mentally ill during the course of the trial, his mother was assessed to be just fine. She refused to comment on the motives, but it was speculated that a history of domestic abuse at the hands of her husband made her prone to cold-blooded violence. Whether her involvement in the crime was forced or of her own will remains unknown to this day

Conclusion

Over the years, society has progressed a great deal from the time of its inception. Man has risen from its primitive beginnings and forayed into many fields of technological and societal advancement. Notwithstanding the achievements and progress, however, man is often the biggest foe of its own kind.

Of the thousands of murder victims each year, there are a select few who find themselves in the hands of a bloodthirsty cannibal killer. For these killers, the feeling of power and control over another human being becomes intoxicating, and their victims undergo an excruciating and torturous death.

The sense of control unfortunately supersedes the moral conscience of these murderers. The derangement of such individuals has led to the untimely loss of many innocent lives. What's more, from the outset, these individuals cannot be differentiated from other human beings. They often have social lives and cannot be distinguished through appearance, or even frequent interaction. Their evil resides beneath the surface, buried deep within years of trauma and childhood abuse, yet it stands ready and willing for its moment to unleash itself upon the perfect victim.

A serial killer lives among humanity and waits in the shadows. They are the manifestation of evil in physical form, embodying the greatest fears and calamities of human kind. They are that part of humanity that exists alongside the common man – the part where the devil truly rules.

About the Author

Stephanie Brannon is a true crime writer from Lubbock, Texas. Her passion for writing and researching about criminal psychology and serial murder led her to become the 2016 winner of the Little Bear Journalism Award for true crime. Stephanie is a self-proclaimed "nerd" with an avid fascination into the macabre. She describes her writing as exploring "the darkest regions of the human mind," and delivering "quick shots to the heart." Although writing is her main passion, she also enjoys simple pleasures like coffee, artisan bread, and hiking in the wilderness.

Printed in Poland
by Amazon Fulfillment
Poland Sp. z o.o., Wrocław